The Assembly Line
Called Out of Darkness

Erika Danielle

Copyright © 2019 Erika Neal Enterprises LLC
All rights reserved.
Published By: Erika Neal Enterprises LLC

ISBN-13: 9780578479422

This book is dedicated to my son, my little love, Legend Landon. You were the power switch to my assembly line. You changed my life. What an honor it is to be chosen for you. I love you more than you'll ever know. You are my forever blessing, from a phenomenal God, who phenomenally loves.

I love you more.

Mommie.

CONTENTS

Power ON: Called Out of Darkness

Trust God Has A Plan

Take Your Natural Glasses Off

Feed Your Spirit

Don't Dwell On Your Circumstance

Keep Your Praise

Find Purpose

Let The Holy Spirit Work

The Final Assembly

Shipping & Handling: Time To Move

Signed, Sealed, Delivered: Thrive

The Finished Product

ACKNOWLEDGMENTS

- I want to start off by thanking *my mommie,* Marpessa Brown. I couldn't even begin to document everything that you have done for me, let alone me and my child! I would be absolutely nothing without you, The Most High couldn't have blessed me with a more perfect mother! Because you have been an example of constant strength in my life, learned behavior stood tall in the mist of adversity. You have shown me what it is to not only be a woman, but a **REAL MOTHER!** I take my role so seriously because of the role you have played in my life. I am truly the woman I am today because of you. I love you so much mommie. Thank you!

- To my father, Steven Neal, because you have poured so much into me, I had great abundance to pull from. Thank you for planting and watering the seeds of greatness in me, for leading me to The Most High, and for nurturing my walk along the way. I love you Daddie, thank you for standing in the gap.

- The Franklins! Where do I begin, where would we be without y'all for real? I can't thank you two enough!!! Literally from the time I found out I was pregnant, to the multiple chauffeured rides back and forth to Torrance, to multiple doctor's appointments, multiple times a week (that was all Theeddie because Toy never drove lol!) y'all were right there. To Lucky being born, and Toy you came through with the Pack N Play because I was scared to sleep with him in the bed with me. Fast forward to now with him forever being at y'all house, being treated no different than his Cousin-Brothers. I love you guys dearly.

- To my personal prophet Jazmene Alkire! Thank you for your obedience to The Most High, for surrendering yourself as a vessel to be used by Him. He speaks so much into my life through you, and I am forever grateful. I love you dearly.

My Brother from another mother, Chris, thank you for the many conversations, and the countless times you and Jazmene have given me so much unsolicited, but very useful information about everything under the sun-but also for the many times I DID solicit the information...you always came through, always there, always available. Thank you! Although you guys are not physically right by side, y'all have always been right by my side, and appreciate it much! I love you two!

- To the most amazing God Parents in the world, my Uncle Robbie and Auntie Donna! You guys have been a consistent blessing in my life, and since Lucky has been here it's just as if ya'll are his God Parents too! LOL! He lucked up! No seriously, I appreciate you both tremendously, and I am so grateful to call you my God Mother and God Father. Auntie Donna thank you for always making sure that I'm looking right (we won't talk about the natural journey), and Uncle Robbie, I hope you're getting ready to marry me off!!! Lol!

- To the Lewis family. Shante thank you for the great edits, feedback, and the Hebrew callouts ☺ Cortez, being almost famous and all, I appreciate you taking the time to help lil 'ole me bring this book to publication! I greatly appreciate the two of you extending yourselves, your time, and your effort. It means the world to me. I love y'all!

- To the men who stepped in...OMG! I am so blessed! Derek Morgan, Theedie, Jordan Le'Blanc, Kimani Love, ya'll didn't miss a beat, and it hasn't gone unnoticed. We are tremendously blessed, and forever grateful!

- To my Day Ones.... y'all already know! Tammy Johnson, Ashlee Gaddis, and Yushikea Gerez! Man, if don't nobody know the real, y'all do. Every intricate detail, every step of the way. Talk about going through ups and downs together!!! The tears, the laughs, the arguments. The fun, the foolery, and shenanigans. But let's talk about the GROWTH! We have literally grown up together from simple-minded young girls, to some well experienced grown ass women! I am so proud of us, and I couldn't have imagined this journey without y'all. With eighteen years of great history in the books, I look forward to what the next few decades have in store for us. I love you Ladies!

- To my Spirit Mom, Ms. Debra. Although our relationship was very short lived, it made an everlasting impact on me. May you rest in peace love.

- To all my family, my friends, and coworkers who have poured into me, who have sharpened me- knowingly and unknowingly, THANK YOU! Thank you for the countless nights you stayed up talking with me. Thank you for the many text messages, the words of encouragement, the books you've sent me (Auntie Sonya), the bible readings, scriptures, the ghetto but fitting colloquialisms that spoke to my spirit and soul, THANK YOU! Thank you for allowing me to be me! When I was the lost me, the finding my way me, and now the me I'm growing into. THANK YOU! I love you all!!!

- To the ones who played me, crossed me, and wrote me off, THANK YOU! For it was good that I was afflicted.

*When you pass through the waters, I will be with you; and when you pass through the rivers,
they will not sweep over you. When you walk through the fire, you will not be burned;
the flames will not set you ablaze.*

Isaiah 43:2

Power ON

Called Out of Darkness

Then I went down to the potter's house, and, behold, he wrought a work on the wheels. And the vessel that he made of clay was marred in the hand of the potter: so he made it again another vessel, as seemed good to the potter to make it

Jeremiah 18:3-4

In 2013 I went through one of the most heart-breaking times of my life. I found out I was pregnant, and shortly after my then boyfriend walked away from me. I was devastated. Not to mention afraid! What the hell was I going to do with a child? And alone! Heartbroken, embarrassed, and ashamed are just a few words that described my mental, emotional, and spiritual state. Knowing that this baby was here for a reason, I still wrestled with the thought of an abortion. My doctor had offered me a pill that would cause my body to miscarry the child, being that I was only about four weeks when I found out, I could get rid of it and carry on with my life. Who would ever know? But to get rid of it.... that's what I couldn't get past. This was not last night's leftovers that I was taking to the trash, this was my child! A life inside of me that God blessed me with regardless the circumstance! I decided it was time to grow up, I had prayed about being the woman God called me to be and it was time to put my big girl panties on and step into that. I was called to be a mother, and I had to own that whether my child's father stuck around or not! After a long emotional conversation at my older sister's house, I got in my car and decided it was time to speak with the Father. As I drove home, I cried with everything in me, and I said to the Lord "Okay, I am scared. I am hurt beyond measure, but I trust you and whatever is meant to be will be." I was broken, and this would not be the last night of my tears.

Little did I know my state of brokenness was the power switch of the assembly line that would lead me on a journey of self-discovery! Putting away who I thought was me and discovering the real me that God said he knew before I was formed in my mother's womb. (Jeremiah 1:5) I was 27 when I started on this journey and what I knew about myself was, I partied, I liked guys, and I knew how to turn up! But that wasn't me! That couldn't have possibly be all that I was made up of. A cute outfit to hit the streets, some flirty conversation and a few patron shots? Surely there had to be more to me than that!

I was confused! In one minute I was praying to be the woman God had created me to be, telling God I wanted to walk in my purpose, that I wanted more of him and to use me, and in the next minute, I was calling my girlfriends to see what was the next thing we could get into, I was playing house with my boyfriend, and smoking and drinking on a regular basis. The two didn't add up! But God knew what was on the inside of me, he knew what he wanted out of me, and so he catapulted me into my destiny; well, the first steps that would lead me to my destiny. Which meant I had to be broken.

Broken (/ˈbrōkən/)
1. Incomplete
2. Being in a state of disarray; disordered.

To be spiritually broken, one is humbled unto Yahuah and completely surrendered to him for spiritual growth and maturity while in a state of disarray and disorder. It is then if allowed, God uses your brokenness to cultivate and maximize what he has planted inside of you. For your brokenness was never designed to overcome you, but to push you into your divine destiny. The bible says, "The steps of a good man are ordered by the Lord: and he delighteth in his way" (Ps. 37:23) Therefore, God is ordering your steps, and sometimes, for those of us who are a little more strong willed, God must take us through a path of brokenness to subdue our will to his. But be not afraid, for the bible says, "The Lord is close to the brokenhearted and saves those who are crushed in spirit." (Ps. 34:18)

Over the next couple years my brokenness took me through about ten different phases or stages of spiritual growth. Spiritual growth that was needed in order to lead me into my destiny. So, while everything seemed like it was out of whack, and falling apart in the natural, God knew exactly what he was doing in the spirit, causing everything to come together. Oftentimes, this is what's happening in our lives when we have no idea what's going on. It's like we believe in God, but we don't understand he has full control over everything that takes place in our lives, whether he allows attacks of the enemy, or if he orchestrates the mess himself. God is sovereign and in complete control.

Over the course of this book I am going to explain how to recognize your brokenness for what it is-the power switch to the assembly line that The Most High has placed you on. The Assembly Line is your place for spiritual growth through a sequence of spiritual workstations. You will find key steps needed to stay right where you need to be, and to become the you God originally created. I will help you work through exactly what I did to remain in the Father's presence and on His radar, while showing you what was going on in my natural life at each spiritual workstation. Understand it has taken me a total of three years to fully complete this book because in order to write about it, I had to first live it. This has been a process, and it will be a process for you. Some of these phases you may not understand until years after the first time you read this. But do the work. The process will work itself out.

My prayer is that you will begin to see things deeper than what appears on the surface. That you cling to God mightily, take these steps serious, and document your own journey to discovery and destiny.

Be Blessed.

Workstation 1

TRUST THAT GOD HAS A PLAN

Sure, we've heard over and over throughout our lives that God has a plan for our lives, and this is very true. But when you're living your life not necessarily lined up with the word or God's will for your life, nine times out of ten you're not thinking about the plan God has for you. When I was doing what I wanted to do, the idea of God's plan for my life was not something I pondered on daily because in my mind I thought I was outside of whatever it was God had for me and sooner or later I would line up. Not realizing that even when you are out of order you're still within his plan. There is nothing we do that takes God by surprise, absolutely nothing. So, while you're out living your life and not really concerning yourself with the things of God, or even when you're partially concerning yourself with the things of God-God still has it all under control. He's already taken this into account.

God knew it wasn't going to be until I hit this low point in my life that I would start questioning what was going on and really looking to him for insight and a plan. And that's normally what happens isn't it? It's like we're living how we want, and that could range from completely out of control to straddling the fence...and we all know the straddlers-like myself, praying for one thing in the Lord but living a completely different lifestyle, all the while attending church on Sunday. Either way it's not until things have gotten completely beyond our control, all hell has broken loose and we no longer have a handle on the things we once did, that we start to really turn to The Most High to see what it is that's going on. Automatically us Christian folk like to blame the devil, "oh this is an attack of the enemy" and that could very much be so, but it could also be God rearranging some things to get your butt in line. He is God and being the sovereign God that he is, he knew and knows

exactly what it's going to take to get your tail to seek him. Which is ultimately what he wants from all his children. He wants us to seek him, lean on him, and let him guide us in all of our ways because....
GOD HAS A PLAN!

So, the plan for my life never included me being a baby momma! Nothing against the other baby mommas in the world, I just never thought in a million years that I would end up one of them. I mean come on, I just knew I was a girl that would get married, have a few good years with my husband to travel and just be alone before we even thought about kids. My child's father and I had even talked about that, talked about places we wanted to go and things we wanted to do. I mean I had it all planned out. I wanted to be married and happily settled in my marriage before I started popping out babies, but let's be real we also weren't using any type of protection when we were having sex- so the possibility of children before marriage was very real and it gave way for the opportunity for God to take my life in a different direction than what I had previously planned. Now let's get one thing straight, nothing takes God by surprise, but that doesn't mean he can only do things one way in your life. Yes, he sets the end from the beginning, but it doesn't mean he can't do things, in that middle period, a million different ways to get to that expected end. My child with "baby daddy" may have been evitable, but he could have possibly arrived under different circumstances had I been aligned with God's will in the first place. However, like I said even when you're out of order your steps are still accounted for, you may just have to take a longer, maybe even a little more painful route to get to the end, but you will get there.

How long will it take you to get to the end? Well that's completely up to you. We've already stated that God has a plan, but even in your brokenness you still have the options to either fall in line or do what you want to do. God is never going to force his will on us. He will create situations and circumstances to try to push us back in the right direction, but ultimately, we still have the choice to line up or not. This is where your trust comes in. How much do you really love the Lord? Do you love him enough to trust him? If you realize things are out of control, are you able to sit down and tell your father in heaven that you are leaving things in his hands and actually take yourself out of the problem? Are you able to give up control even when you see an opportunity to make a move? Can you just stand when the Lord tells you to be still and stand? That's putting it all in God's hands and following his plan. Typically, when things get chaotic in our lives, we immediately go into damage control and fix whatever we can.... or think we can. When in actuality, oftentimes that is making things worse because it still may not fall in line with what God has planned.

Now here I am a few months into my pregnancy. My child's father and I are going back and forth dealing with each other. Although when I told him I was pregnant, and his reaction was completely negative, he then flipped on me and seemed okay with it. Then we went a few weeks without speaking at all because he no longer wanted to have a child right then. Then he returned. So, we were constantly up and down. Arguing, then getting along. Talking, then not talking. I was on an emotional rollercoaster with him. I didn't want to stress out the baby, but I couldn't help but to feel stressed with all the back and forth nonsense. Yet the idea of him not being around for our child caused me to deal with his inconsistency even more, hoping he would just get to a point where he accepted that the child was coming; that didn't happen. One day while sitting at my desk listening to a sermon from Bishop T.D. Jakes, God spoke to me very clearly and told me to "leave it alone, stop trying to be God of the situation." That was it. Clear as day, his spoken word. And I did just that. Two days later my child's father texted me to come meet him at a park to talk, I told him I was on my way to bible study, he laughed and said he'll talk to me next year maybe, and I haven't heard from him since. Although it was very challenging, the word I received from God was more important to me than my feelings or anyone else's' opinion. But I believe God's will shall be done, and manifest in our lives exactly how it's supposed to.

I told The Most High back when I was four weeks that I trusted him and whatever happened from there happened. No, I didn't like what The Most High told me, no I don't like that I haven't heard from my child's father, or that he wasn't there when I gave birth, or at my child's first birthday, but if The Most High said it, then so shall it be.

We don't always understand why things happen, we don't always understand why The Most High takes us in certain directions, but sometimes it's not for us to understand. We just have to trust in God and be willing and ready to move when he says move.

You must make a strong decision to trust God. Take a moment to not only evaluate your circumstance but evaluate yourself as well. Be real with yourself! This is the time that you lay it all out there. All future movements will be dependent on what you decide now.

How are you feeling right now? What is your current emotional state?

_____
_____
_____
_____
_____
_____
_____
_____

After assessing the circumstance, what are the best- and worst-case scenarios?

_____
_____
_____
_____
_____
_____
_____
_____

Do you have the ability to change it? If so, would that make it better or worse?

_____
_____
_____
_____
_____
_____
_____
_____

Do you have enough faith to believe that God has a plan for your life?

_____
_____
_____
_____
_____
_____
_____
_____

Do you trust God's sovereignty over your situation? What are you looking for him to do?

_____
_____
_____
_____
_____
_____
_____
_____

Affirmation:

Father I trust you, I know I am in the center of your will for my life.

Stand On IT!

Trust in the LORD with all thine heart; and lean not unto thine own understanding. In all thy ways acknowledge him, and he shall direct thy paths.

Proverbs 3:5-6

Workstation 2

Take Your Natural Glasses Off: Get a Spiritual Perspective

One thing we must understand is that our lives are based on a spiritual realm that we do not see. Everything that is visible to us in the natural was first made so in the spirit realm. Everything. Including the battle that you are facing right now. The bible tells us specifically "for we wrestle not against flesh and blood, but against the rulers of the darkness of this world, against spiritual wickedness in high places." (Ephesians 6:12) Basically meaning the problems we face, and the battles we fight first started in the spiritual realm and then made manifest in the natural realm. Which means there is no way you can fight a spiritual war with a natural perspective. By attempting to do so, you won't be able to get past the offenses that were done to you and the people who hurt you. In order to progress and win, you have to be able to get past that. What you need to understand off top is that this is a war. God placed you here to accomplish something, he created you with a plan in mind, a purpose for you to fulfill. So, understand that the enemy wants by any means necessary, to keep you from fulfilling that purpose. But here's the deal, you are already victorious because the enemy really has no power over you, unless you allow yourself to be defeated. The only way you can be defeated, is if you don't fight. Are you going to let your circumstances over power you, control you, and take over your life and your very well being? No! Why should you? Your circumstance is just that.... a circumstance, it will change. Everything changes eventually. So, in the mean time you put on the full armor of God and you fight for life! You fight for your family, you fight for your ministry and you fight for you territory. Don't give way to the enemy when God has clearly placed you over his head. Don't sell yourself short like that. You can't be a coward your whole life! At some point you have to get some fire under your belly and fight!

     I was five and a half months pregnant when I stopped hearing from my child's father and I was very hurt, very confused, and completely mind blown. I would have never thought in a million years that he would do something like that to me. Never. I was totally disappointed in him, I was mad at him, and honestly a part of me wanted something bad to happen to him. He had morphed into a totally different person. Before we stopped speaking, the contact we did have was always so up and down, I never knew who I was going to be talking to when I did talk to him, or what person he was going to be when I met up with him. So, I prayed. One night after waking up from a deep nap to ridiculous text messages from him, I prayed. I said, "God what is wrong with him? Why is he actin like this, I mean this is unreal." It wasn't just him tripping, it was a very unsettling undertone in those messages, something that just didn't sit right in my spirit. I was laying in my bed and God calmly answered, "It's a spirit." Then the Lord began to show me that the spirit within him was conflicting with the spirit that's in me...His spirit. But that was still kind of hard to understand. I had so many questions. Why were our spirits just now starting to conflict? We were never equally yoked so what's the issue now? I didn't understand fully so I kept what God said in the back of my mind. I tried to leave it at just a spiritual issue, but I couldn't. It was sill all very natural to me.

Then it dawned on me, I needed to change my glasses. I was so caught up in what was going on that I couldn't see the spiritual aspect working behind the scenes. I talked to my father about it one day over tea, and he told me God didn't have to answer all my questions, I just needed to trust him. Trust his word and know there are spiritual implications to every action. But it's like honestly who wants to hear that while you're in the middle of a life altering circumstance? Of course, he was right, but I wasn't in tune with what was going on in the spirit because the natural seemed so much more real. It was real, my pain was real, my heartache was real, my fear was real... or so I thought. For a while I went back and forth on whether or not I heard what I actually heard from The Most High.

Did God really say that or was I just making up excuses for his behavior? It was very hard for me to blame everything on the "spiritual realm" especially when talking to other people about what was going on. Sure enough, I would have sounded crazy telling them "oh the devil made him do it." Lol, who was going for that? When in fact, it wasn't that the devil made him do anything, but he certainly used him. Same way he used me when I spat out the things, I said to him in anger. The fact was we had both been used by the enemy all a part of his ploy, but only first allowed by God because he had a plan.

The truth is most of us go along through life without ever really stopping and paying attention to the spirit realm that projects the details in our natural lives. We've already established that the spirit realm is the causal realm, so we would think it would make sense to be in tune with what's going on in the spirit. But honestly speaking because we cannot see the spirit realm it makes it hard for that to stay a focal point of ours, when our natural lives seem so much more real. I totally understand that, and felt the exact same way until my situation caused me to view things differently. See, a broken state in your life will cause you to question and reevaluate everything you thought you already knew. You need answers and you go on a trip, a long journey to find them. Yet the only person you're going to get any real answers and understanding from is God. There is not a man walking this earth, or any other force you can conjure up, that can give you the understanding, reassurance, and comfort that the The Most High can.

You can stay up with your girlfriends drinking wine and talking about issues all night, you can cry to your sisters and your mother until your head hurts, and you still won't get what you're looking for. You will still walk away feeling just as lost as you did before, if not more confused. Yes, these people in your life love you and they may feel for you and they may wish and want things to get better for you, but they can't do anything about it for you. Some will try, and that's out of love of course, their hearts are in the right place, but it still won't leave you settled. You must seek God in your brokenness. There is no way you can seek God without tuning into the spirit realm, no way. The deeper you go with God the more in tune you will get, and little by little it will all start to slowly make sense to you. The Most High will began to show you more, he will take you deeper, higher, and in doing so the spirt becomes more natural than your natural. However, for most people this is not an overnight process, so be patient, and be obedient. The more time spent with The Most High, the more obedience is required from you, and I'll tell you now, obedience is key.

I'm not promising or saying that God is going to make everything crystal clear to you because he won't. God does not really operate like that, and the more you get into his word, and develop your relationship with him, you'll find this to be very true. This can be challenging, at least for me it was. I wanted to know exactly what was going on and why, and I wanted to know what the outcome would be. I still don't have that answer and I'm a few years in this thing, although the purpose is much clearer. God won't make everything crystal clear, but he will give you what you need exactly when you need it. God has a way of giving you revelation into the things around you, and I've found for myself with revelation comes peace. A sense of a peace like "oh okay, I got this," and you could still be right in the middle of your hell, but you'll have just enough for that particular moment in hell.

I have people tell me to this very day they don't know how I do it. I don't get too upset when talking about my son's father. Do I have an opinion of him and his actions...? Sure, I do, and it's not a Godly one either! But I am also very aware of the fact that none of this would be going on had God not allowed it. It does not change the situation, and it doesn't necessarily make the situation itself better, but it makes it easier for me to handle. I could have gone about doing things my own way. I could have showed up at his doorstep every day. Called him repeatedly cursing him out and telling him what type of person he is...but I didn't. Where would that have gotten me or my son? Now don't get me wrong, it wasn't just because I'm so mature that I didn't do those things, it's because God spoke to me with clear instructions, and he graced me with the ability to follow them. What was I supposed to do after that? I had no choice but to tuck my tail, take my eyes off the natural and shift focus into what was going on in the spirit realm, as challenging as it was to me.

Some days are better than others. I can go lengthy periods of time when I am completely tuned in to God and the path, he has me on, and I am unmoved by what's going on around me. Then there are times when I'm like you know what, I'm tired of this, I'm ready to throw in the towel because I can't deal any more. But that, my friend, is all a part of the journey and our walk with The Messiah. The most important thing is that you get back in line, get back into the word, and line back up with The Most High's will for your life.

Tuning into the spirit realm requires daily communion with God. You need to be praying, reading, and spending time with God some way or another. Consistent communion with the The Most High, allows you to be more sensitive to the voice of God, learning how he speaks to you, and it also strengthens your discernment, and ability to decipher what's going on spiritually. The more sensitive you are to the spirit the more in tune you will be. At this point, God will begin to reveal things to you, and it may no longer just be about your current situation. He may begin to speak to you about where he is taking you- and once God starts showing you that (which is one of my favorites lol) you'll start to see why you had to go through what you are presently going through or gone through. So, it's almost as if you get a two for one! And who doesn't love a great deal?

As time went on for me, God spoke to me very little concerning what I was actually going through. There was very little explanation given, he still hasn't shown me or given me answers to certain prayers concerning my son or his father, but he started speaking to me a lot about where he was taking me. See we must understand that God is not just focused on our present situation, and that's because this situation didn't catch God by surprise. He knew this was going to be something we went through just like he knows it's going to be something we make it out of. So, he's more like, "come on, let's go, you can't stop right here there's more in store for you". That's the mentality you must have as well. This is not the end baby! There is so much more ahead of you if you keep tugging. I don't care what you have to do: if you have to listen to the same song over and over on repeat throughout the day, if you have to take more breaks than a smoker to go pray throughout the day, if you have to cry and call on Jesus every night- just keep walking! The Most High will see you through. "He that began a good work in you will perfect it until the day of Christ Jesus." (Philippians 1:6 nasb)

Beginning with prayer to The Most High, ask God to reveal to you the things that you want to see. Ask God to give you a spiritual perspective, seeing into things deeper than what appears on the surface.

Are you able to recognize the spiritual forces behind the scenes?

What spiritual things are you discerning?

How has being able to see spiritually changed your natural perspective?

_____
_____
_____
_____
_____
_____
_____
_____

Are you able to find peace in your current circumstance being able to put things in the proper perspective?

_____
_____
_____
_____
_____
_____
_____
_____

How has tuning into the spirit helped you the most?

_____
_____
_____
_____
_____
_____
_____
_____

Affirmation:

I walk by faith, not by sight.

The Assembly Line

Stand On IT!

For we wrestle not against flesh and blood, but against principalities, against powers, against the rulers of the darkness of this world, against spiritual wickedness in high places.

Ephesians 6:12

Workstation 3

Feed Your Spirit

My daddy always uses this really great analogy when referring to feeding your spirit. He's constantly telling us how important it is for believers to feed our spirits daily just as we do our natural bodies. He says, "you don't give your body one to two meals a week and expect it run off that, so why do you only feed your spirit man on a Sunday and maybe a mid-week meal?" Basically saying, the word of God is our food. Which the scriptures tell us that explicitly, "Man shall not live on bread alone, but on every word that proceedeth out of the mouth of God." (Matthew 4:4) The word is what powers us, it builds our spirit man and causes our flesh to die. So, if you're doing just the opposite, how do you expect to come out of your situation as a victor? We have got to feed our inner man on a daily basis, and this can even sometimes come down to a minute by minute thing.

I'll use myself as an example. I love music, I am a music person. So, when I'm at work if I'm not listening to a good word, I'll have my headphones in, doing my stuff vibing to some great music. Now which music I'm listening to is the problem though. Every morning when I sit down at my desk I turn on my bible app, listen to about five chapters of whatever book I'm in for the day, and then I turn on some gospel to get my day started. Typically, around 10-10:30 I'm ready to turn the gospel off and vibe to something else. This always becomes a challenge because if I don't choose carefully I will slowly start to revert back to some of my old ways of thinking- just that quick. Now I know some of you are like sure whatever, but I'm telling you this walk of righteousness is a minute by minute thing! It is no joke. So, if I go three days of listening to Beyoncé, YG, and Drake radio on Pandora, sure enough by the weekend I'm ready to turn up and get into some of the old things I used to do.

This is just me being honest. Oppose to if I choose to maybe switch up my gospel station and maybe just turn on some Lecrae and Mali Music if I don't want traditional gospel, and from there I might turn on a sermon or two- and by the weekend I'm straight. No biggie, everything is still in order. It all comes down to, what you are feeding your inner man? If your inner man is not being fed, how do you expect to be strong in battle? And please believe there is a battle going on daily for you. What side are you helping?

When you're in a state of brokenness, ultimately the goal is to move past whatever circumstance you've found yourself in that caused your current condition and draw nearer to the Creator who allowed this circumstance for a purpose. Along the way throughout that journey you have got to feed your spirit. You have to build up your inner man because that situation can beat you down daily. You are in a fight for your life! For your health, for your family, for your ministry and for your destiny. There are two players in the game, God our creator who wants to give you life, and turn your negative into a positive...and the enemy who wants to capitalize on your negative and make the situation even worse. It is up to you which team you are going to fight on along the way. You can feed life to your life, to your spirt, to your environment. Or you can feed yourself death.

Speak life into your situation. My dad told me these exact words while I was going through, "speak life to your circumstance, it won't be easy, but it will be fulfilling." And I remember thinking, how in the world will it be fulfilling? Boy have I been surprised! It truly is. When you start speaking positively over your circumstance. When you're in God's word, reading and studying, praising and worshipping you begin to focus on the bigger picture...GOD- The Most High! You begin to see that God is not going to let you fail, regardless of how it looks, who hurt you, or whatever. When you shift your perspective and begin to build your spirit by feeding on God's words of life, you begin to see that although I am going through hell right now, I serve a God that's bigger and more powerful than this. Trust me, he has a word for you right when you need it, if you just keep your focus on him. When you stay emerged in what God is saying, whether it be in his book, or a message by your pastor, of if he's speaking directly to you, you start to look forward to your next move, the next word he has for you. It actually becomes quite exciting, and little by little he will walk alongside of you, right out of that hell hole you're in.

While I was pregnant and alone, I stayed listening to messages and reading scripture. Like I mentioned earlier I would turn on my messages at work, I would literally pray and ask God to direct me while I was browsing YouTube. I would listen to T.D Jakes, Juanita Bynum, Bishop Tudor Bismark, and whoever else the Lord led me to listen to. I was feeding my spirit, and it was soooo necessary. It was almost as if I was hooked. I had to submerge myself in God's word because my thoughts and fears were so loud in my head that I had to have something to drown them out. I needed something else to focus on. It's so easy to get caught up in our situation, pondering on the 'what if' type of questions, thinking of all the possible outcomes- and more often than not the negative outcomes are the main focus. Which is so unhealthy. It is not helping you mentally, spiritually, and especially not emotionally, when you're sitting up letting your imagination run wild fueling your fears. That's a scary place to be.

When you notice your thoughts getting to be too much, becoming overwhelming or even when they're just too negative, that's when you need to call on the The Most High. Pray, break your bible out, turn some gospel on, pull up a sermon on YouTube- something! But you have got to feed your spirit. The more you feed your spirit when you notice you're dwelling on the all the negative things in your life, the more it will become like second nature to you. Your inner man, your spirit man, will then begin to crave the word of God. Just like food cravings it will become stronger and stronger, and you'll keep feeding your spirit, and building your spirit up and before you know it a negative thought will come to mind, or you'll be mid conversation with someone, and you'll start quoting scripture and wondering when you learned it! Lol! You'll begin to shock yourself.

For me this made my walk with God more and more real. When I would be talking to someone, even during my own issue, I could be encouraging someone else and scripture would just flow out my mouth, and in those moments, I would be like wow! My God is real and can't nobody tell me otherwise. Without me realizing it or writing a scripture down and memorizing it, scripture was just embedded in my soul from all the "food' I had been giving it.

Feeding your spirit is the most important thing you can do when you find yourself in a broken state. Meditating on God's word, whether it was a word spoken directly to you, a message you heard, or a prophecy, meditate on it. Seek God out about it, get some clarity and insight, and rest in it.

While I was pregnant every word that was spoken to me, I wrote it down. If I didn't have something to write it down with right away, I would try my hardest to remember it and write down what I remembered when I got home. This was before I started keeping a pen and pad in my purse. Sometimes I prayed over the words and sometimes I didn't. Sometimes I asked God to reveal more, or give me clarity, or just to speak more in depth about the word and sometimes I didn't. Sometimes I would get a little more from God regarding the word and sometimes he would say nothing else about it. All of it has been a part of my walk. It has caused me to trust God more, it's caused me to discern the words I get from other people, and to discern and trust when I'm hearing God speak to me directly. That's why it is important that you keep walking. All this that you are going through is a part of a bigger picture. For you on a personal level, and how you fit into God's bigger plan altogether. You are on the assembly line.

In any case we are all soldiers for the Lord. No matter what emotional state we're in, or where we are in our journey with God, and what's going on in our life-we're all going to face spiritual warfare and in order to fight properly, our spirt has got to be healthy and ready for battle. You don't put a weak and hungry man in the middle of a war and expect to him to fight for his life and for the lives of the people around him. So why would you expect to be able to fight at your fullest capacity with a weak and hungry spirit? Look at it this way, in most of our cases, some form of spiritual warfare has landed us in the situation we are currently in; in our broken emotional, financial, or spiritual state- now God has called us to retreat (which is why you may feel alone as if no one understands) to give you a hiding place to build your spirit. To feed and to grow you, so you can get back out on the field stronger than ever. The key to getting your strength back is maximizing this "downtime" and taking full advantage of what the The Most High is trying to do in your life. You're able to do that by spending time in God's word, praying, and just sitting in your quiet space at The Most High's feet. During this time God will speak into your life, and into your situation- giving you clarity, strategy, and insight into the thing happening around you. He will give you nuggets of encouragement letting you know that you are on the right path and direction for your next step.

While I was in my first semester of ministry school, my instructor broke down several different disciplines' believers should include in their lives. Some of these disciplines are daily and others may be weekly, or even occasionally, but the purpose of each discipline is to become closer to God in different ways. These disciplines are also a means of feeding your spirit. One discipline you can include in your daily life to bring you closer to God and build your inner man is daily prayer time. Most people find praying in the morning before they start their day to be very beneficial for the day. To go to the Father and set their day, getting direction, instruction and their assignments for that day. It's like going to the Father and getting a direct download, almost like a head's up with guidance. However, if a morning devotion is a little difficult, then you set a time that's best for you. The point is making the time and getting your prayer in.

Another discipline to include in your weekly schedule is fasting. Fasting is a good way to connect with The Most High on a deeper level, while getting control over your flesh. You can pick a day out of the week and commit to fasting the whole day or committing to a time frame throughout the day that will work for you. Take it slow, begin with a fast that you know you can do. I began with mid-day fasting from the time I woke up until noon. I than moved to a sun up to sun down fast, and finally full 24 hour fast. The point is the commitment and to set aside time to connect with the spirit.

Just know that in the middle of battle going hungry is probably one of the most detrimental things that could happen. You wouldn't do it in your natural life, so don't starve your spirit. When your spirit is nourished and constantly full off God's word you become more sensitive to the spirit, and your discernment will become stronger. You will also become more sensitive to God's voice which will serve as direction and guidance during this time, and throughout your life.

Feeding your spirit is the most important thing you can do for yourself at every step of your walk. It's one of those things that you never do away with. It's how you will continually tap deeper into the things of God. It is how you build your spirit man up, train, and prepare for battle.

What are some of the ways that you feed your spirit? Do you have any favorites?

_____
_____
_____
_____
_____
_____
_____
_____

Since regularly feeding your spirit man, what changes have you seen in yourself? (Do you know more scripture? Do you find yourself talking about God more?) Are you seeing effects of the time you've been spending in God's word?

_____
_____
_____
_____
_____
_____
_____
_____

Building your spirit generally causes a stronger desire to go deeper into the things of the Lord. Do you find yourself wanting to more, what are your craving from The Most High right now?

_____
_____
_____
_____
_____
_____
_____
_____

Now that you're consistently building your spirit, are you more aware of things that negatively trigger you? What have you noticed to be some immediate spirit triggers?

_____
_____
_____
_____
_____
_____
_____
_____

Keeping in mind that this is a battle, what are some ways that you can better guard your spirit?

_____
_____
_____
_____
_____
_____
_____
_____

Affirmation:

I do not live on bread alone, but on every word that comes from the mouth of The Most High God.

Stand On IT!

My son, if you receive my words and treasure up my commandments with you, making your ear attentive to wisdom and inclining your heart to understanding; yes, if you call out for insight and raise your voice for understanding, if you seek it like silver and search for it as for hidden treasures, then you will understand the fear of the Lord and find knowledge of God

Proverbs 2:1-22

Workstation 4

Don't Dwell on the Situation

I get it. I know this is hard, it's a challenge to not think about what you are currently going through. What you're feeling, and all the many possible outcomes you've come up with in your own mind. I get it. Trust me I was there. No matter what I did, or what I was doing I could easily find myself drifting off thinking about everything that happened. It was as if I couldn't control it. It was so easy for me to try to go back and replay everything that I could possibly remember that happened between the two of us. I beat myself down trying to think of signs that I possibly overlooked, signs that if I would have just paid closer attention to, this all could have possibly been avoided. Thoughts that were starting to drive me crazy. Literally. I was driving myself nuts wondering about the what ifs, wishing I could change some things, and making up the outcome aside from what God said.

All this does is make things worse and let me tell you how. When you get to sitting up thinking about the past, thinking about ways you maybe could have avoided the situation you're in now, and ways this thing could play out....you get outside of God. There's no way you can be focused on God and God's will if you're totally consumed with your own thoughts. How does that work? More than likely, at this point, your thoughts are not lining up with God's will for you, and they're surely not lining up with what God thinks. We don't even think on God's level when we're spiritually strong, so we're definitely not thinking anywhere near his level when we're going through a breaking process. But that's fine. So, this is what God does. He shows you or gives you the end from the beginning and tells you to walk it out. Now when you're supposed to be walking, if you're sitting around pre-consumed with your situation, you ain't walking. Most importantly you're not doing whatever it is

God wants you to be doing right now. This is another tactic of the enemy. Remember Satan can't make us do anything, but he can plant seeds, he can make us start to focus so much on ourselves that we aren't focusing on God and what God wants.

In my personal experience, that's when my mouth would do a little more talking than I would have liked. When I was sitting up in my feelings, thinking about how poor and pitiful I was, that was when it was easiest for me to start bad mouthing my sons' father, or saying things I really didn't mean. Nevertheless, they were powerful words spoken, and ultimately still had the power to affect my situation. Remember our words have power and have the ability to shape our lives. You see how that all works? Tricky little thing isn't it. You get to thinking about you. Indulging in your thoughts, wallowing in your feelings, and next thing you know, here you go speaking things that have power to negatively impact your situation. Because nine times out of ten if you've been entertaining a pity party all day, your words are not going to be that positive.

I remember times I would find myself looking at my infant child and just feeling so sad. I felt so bad that he would have to grow up without his father because I chose the wrong one. It hurt me to the core thinking about having to have the conversation with him when he asked me where his father was. It was the one thing that bothered me the most about the whole situation, his feelings. How would he feel, would he suffer from abandonment issues, would he grow up and be a fatherless black boy statistic? All of this would play on my mind day in and day out and it just made me so sad- wrapped up in strength and a smile by the way, because Lord forbid people knew how I really felt! It was just too much, and it all was eating away at me little by little every day. I was trying my hardest not to slip into a state of depression for the sake of my child, but my goodness how much could one take?

I didn't realize at that time that my biggest problem was me. I was so focused on me that I wasn't focused on God, and that is how we begin to dwell. See in the very beginning when I said, "I'm going to trust you God." I really didn't know then how deep this thing would get, and I was at a point where trusting Him was becoming a little too challenging- I mean if we're being real. See because now my feelings were involved a bit deeper than they were when I was 4 weeks pregnant, because now my child was looking back at me in the flesh. Now it was really real! And what I felt at those moments when I looked at my son, felt more real than the God who said He had me.

But God!

One night I was laying in my bed, I had just finished praying, and was just lying there in the dark, which I did often during those times. I received a message from my father telling me to cast down thoughts that arose against the word of the Lord, and to bring them under the authority of The Most High. Wow was that powerful, and much needed. And although I didn't know if there was a particular way to do this, I began to put it into practice as it came to my remembrance, every time a negative thought, or any mood-altering thought would come to mind. I would simply say, "I cast down that thought, and bring it under the authority of the living God." It was difficult at first because I wouldn't remember to do it, and out of pure humanistic habits, it was much easier and comforting to dwell in my thoughts and feelings. As I continued to speak this command, I noticed over time it would lighten my mood, and no sooner than I would make the command, the thought would be gone. The more and more I practiced this, the more and more I began to look back to God, and got out of myself.

Noticing how well this worked, and now being in a better and happier mood more often than not, I started to go back to previous words I had received from the Lord. I would read them, pray over them, meditate on them and straight up just talk to God about them. It was like a release for me, and I began to look forward to the next word. I was straight up addicted to hearing from God! Trust me this was a much better place than listening to the thoughts of the enemy playing over and over in my head like a broken record player.

No matter what the situation is, there is always something else that you could be focusing on, right? For me I had to make myself think about all the joy my new baby was going to bring me. When I would find myself slipping away, or sometimes I would have already been there- then I would have to change the channel. You have control over what you want to think about. If you notice you're thinking about something that doesn't make you happy, or makes you feel sad and low- bring it under The Most High's authority and change your thought. It's that simple.

I had noticed that whenever I would get off the freeway coming into Long Beach, I would immediately start to feel sad, thinking about my ex and what we used to ride around the city doing. It was crazy! Like I don't know if that is classified as a stronghold or not, but that's certainly what it felt like. So, I would absolutely have to refocus. I mean I live in Long Beach, almost everything I do is in Long Beach, there is no way I was going to continue walking around sad thinking about my ex, and what went wrong all the time. So, I would think about other things. Don't get me wrong it's hard to shift your thoughts sometimes- but it can be done.

Turn on some music, gospel is always a good way to change your mood. I love singing, so I would turn on some music that I could sing along too and that would boost me up instantly. Another good way to release unwanted thoughts is to offer them up to The Most High in prayer. As soon as you find yourself drifting, when you feel your mood changing, when you notice, because sometimes we don't recognize the drift, that you're in that place, start praying. Do what my Grandfather calls a breath prayer, and quietly give the thought to the Lord, and command your thoughts to come under the authority of Yahua Elohim. Again, when you're drifting into a negative space, that is never of God, and he does not want you to be there, let alone stay there, so bring it under his authority.

When you're here, you also must do some self-evaluation. You must be able to check yourself and be real with you. I say that because the fact of the matter is some people like to sit up and wallow. Some people like to be upset, sad, and depressed. Some people like to be the victim, whether it's learned behavior, something they're used to because of past experiences, I don't know, but I know whatever the reason is, you must overcome it. Just like anything else, overcoming is all about changing your mind set. Again- give it to God. Recognizing that some things for some of us, we just don't have to the power to do in our own strength. Our Heavenly Father knows this, and that's why he constantly tells us that he is our strength. Some of us are trying to walk things out in natural strength that in reality we're absolutely too weak for, and that's just the flat-out truth.

I can honestly tell you throughout this whole journey people have consistently told me, "I don't know how you do it. You handled this so well, I wouldn't have been able to do." Etc., etc. and I always follow up it, "It is only by the grace of God." Like are you kidding me? I didn't walk this out in my strength. I didn't not go crazy because of my own might. I just told y'all that I literally would have immediate thoughts of my son's father as soon as I got off the 710 freeway, daily! Those thoughts would run rampant in my mind, I felt like I was going freaking stir crazy. BUT GOD! He said, NOT SO! That is his power, not mine! That is why it's a must that you don't dwell, you give it to him immediately, turn your praise music on, and you praise the name of Yahuah, and let him do his thing. Trust me, you'll be like me, five years later not even knowing how you got through without a chip on your shoulder. You won't even be thinking about what you overcame, until someone brings it up to you. As if it was a walk in the park. That is God's grace, his power, his strength! Rest in it! Allow him to step in, give it to him and keep it pushing.

Hallelujah! I felt that. You better walk!

Again, you cannot keep walking if you keep stopping. It's that simple. Now don't get me wrong, you can stop along the way, and you will stop along with the way, but you cannot dwell. Stop, shed some tears, pray, curse, shout, but release, give it to God, and get back on your path. I encourage you to keep pushing. Do not get stuck in the pain, and more than anything do not get stuck in the anger. The pain will demobilize you, and the anger will kill you from the inside out- LITERALLY. You have got to keep trucking. You cannot afford to get stuck, there is someone waiting on you.

You have no time to dwell, there is still a lot to be done, and this journey has just begun. However, trust me it's going to get much more fun, and you'll begin to see why you had to go through what you went through. I know it sounds crazy now, but you will be grateful.

So, get up, let's keep going sweetheart.

We're humans, and we are not divine in any of our ways. It's easy to get caught up in our feelings and if we're honest, sometimes it's really comforting to stay there. However, we already established that dwelling on what has happened to us is in no way a positive contributor to your journey. Take a moment to reflect on some of your deepest concerns and write out a few counteracting prayers.

What are some of the negative thoughts that haunt you regarding your situation?

_____
_____
_____
_____
_____
_____
_____
_____

What scares you the most?

_____
_____
_____
_____
_____
_____
_____
_____

When these negative thoughts come to mind, what are some ways you're learning to counteract them?

_____
_____
_____
_____
_____
_____
_____
_____

Have you been successful in this approach? If no, have you identified other alternatives to try?

_____
_____
_____
_____
_____
_____
_____
_____

At this point in your journey, what are some things that you are noticing within yourself? (Spiritually, Emotionally, and Mentally)

_____
_____
_____
_____
_____
_____
_____
_____

Affirmation:

It is well with my soul!

The Assembly Line

Stand On IT!

Finally, brothers and sisters, whatever is true, whatever is noble, whatever is right, whatever is pure, whatever is lovely, whatever is admirable, - if anything is excellent or praiseworthy- think about such things.

Philippians 4:8

Workstation 5

Keep Your Praise!

Honestly this has come to be one of my most favorite things to do! What is that you ask? Praise The Most High! I cannot begin to tell you how much I love singing praises, and partly because I just have a love for singing, so combine that with how much I love Jesus, and I literally have a match made in heaven. Now due to the fact The Most High didn't see it fit to bless me with the gift of a great singing voice, I have a voice that only He can love! But it's enough to gain his attention and draw his presence at my most needed times, and that's exactly what he wants all of us to do.

I know you've probably heard it time and time again, and this may sound like a broken record to you, but here it is again, **PRAISE IS ONE OF YOUR MOST POWERFUL WEAPONS!!!** You can never go wrong when you keep your praise. Worship brings a deeper connection to God. Remember earlier we mentioned when you get stuck dwelling on your circumstance, it's usually because you've taken the focus off the Lord, and placed it on you? Well this is the perfect way to counteract that. Praise can be used to shift your focus, to break through bondages and strongholds, it can lift your mood, and it can break the spirit of depression off you. You can literally draw the spirit of God right there alone in your own home, without stepping foot in a church or church setting, and get everything you need from The Most High. Again, it is one of your most powerful weapons.

Just to quickly examine scriptural reference to music and how it can be used to make moves in the spirit realm, let's look at King Saul and David.

"And it came to pass, when the evil spirit from God was upon Saul, that David took a harp, and played with his hand: so, Saul was refreshed, and was well, and the evil spirit departed from him." (I Samuel 16:23)

So, what is the scripture showing us? Spirits can quickly attach themselves, attack, and/or come up on us to torture us. That's why we must be very careful and mindful of the things we do, the thoughts we think, and just in general the things we're opening ourselves up to. Especially when we're going through a dark time in life. It is absolutely crucial that your guard your spirit, and like I said in an earlier chapter, feed your spirit. Now, because most of the time we find ourselves drawing closer to God, learning more about the spirit realm, and being tuned in to the spirit realm, during this actual wilderness experience, we aren't always aware of the fact that there are probably some spirits already attached to us that have been chilling with us for who knows how long. Spirits that we acquired while we were out doing our own thing, not too much worried about God and what all was going on in the spirit realm. Now, just like those spirits came upon you, they can get off you and flee. However, some spirits require more than a quick breath prayer, laying of the hands, or someone praying over you. Some spirits may need to be played out by music, because music itself is spiritual (which is a whole other topic that'll we'll have to discuss later.)

Just as David came to play his harp which brought peace to Saul's spirit, and stopped the evil spirit from tormenting him; that's the same approach we should take when we are being tormented in our spirit. This is referred to as a Zamar Praise, which simply means making praise to God with instruments. If you're anything like me and don't play an instrument, just find a nice instrumental that you can lift your praise up to The Most High over. We all have a voice in heaven, and although singing along to gospel music is great, there is nothing better than your own stamp being sent to soothe the Father's ears.

I also want you to seriously pay attention to how music is affecting you. The next time you're listening to something, take note of the mood it puts you in, and once you realize it, pay attention to what your spirit is trying to say to you. While you are in the midst of your circumstance, or if you're down right in a state of brokenness, it is not wise to listen to music that will continue to feed that negative, defeated spirit that is trying its best to overtake you.

It took me a minute to realize this, and I know most of you are probably smarter than me so take heed to what I am saying. When my son's father first left, my biggest concern was my unborn child and the things that he would have to endure without his father. That was the abandonment, but after a while heartbreak set in. This was also now a broken relationship, and just like with any other breakup, heartache began to ring aloud. So, what did I do? When I was home alone, I would lie in my bed and listen to slow sappy loves songs about heartbreak. Now as I look back on this, I see how foolish it was of me, but while I was going through, I initially thought nothing of it because music has always been my go-to. I can sit up and listen to music for hours while I'm doing nothing and everything. Little did I realize back then, just how much music resonates in our spirits, whether good or bad, so it is completely up to us to make conscious decisions on what we allow in. Listen to me, music has a way of getting you fuller faster than listening to sermons every day. So, pay attention.

The obvious point here is to get your praise and worship game up. When you get up in the morning and turn on the tv to check the traffic (I don't do this, but I know a lot of people do) turn on Pandora and get you a good gospel station going. I personally prefer Kirk Franklin's or Donnie McClurkin's station but pick one where you know the artist will resonate with your spirit. The objective is to get you in the habit of praise. Get your spirit man accustomed to praising The Most High as soon as you start your day. Thanking him for waking you up and praising him for being who he is- and subconsciously you will have already set your day without you even realizing it.

You will begin to shift your focus from yourself and whatever it is that you're going through or feeling at that time and focus on the Creator of all things. The more and more you focus on God, the bigger He becomes, and the more you come into the realization of not only his power but his sovereignty. Let me tell you, realizing that The Most High is sovereign, is your first step in your now spiritual shift.

Eventually, you will get to the point where waking up and praising will be automatic, and you may not even need to turn on any music to help you. You'll wake up thanking God, singing your adoration and praise, and this is where you ultimately want to be. Your spirit will then be trained to lift and worship our Elohim. What my old pastor used to say, you may have to start off mechanically before it becomes organic. Initially, you, praising The Most High will be something you have to remember to do, kind of train yourself to do, not just in the morning but throughout your day. Eventually, your spiritual desire will be to praise Him, and it will be natural for you.

Here I am five years later, and every morning when I get up I turn on praise and worship music. It has become a habit, to the point where I feel out of sync if I don't do it. I have grown accustomed to waking up, thanking God for waking me, and immediately praising him. I turn the worship music on before my son wakes up because I want the music to get into his spirit as well. On our way to school I don't even let the radio get a chance to come on all the way before I'm making sure the phone is connected and our worship music is playing. I believe this not only sets our day, it ushers in peace in our spirits, which I whole heartedly believe resonates with us throughout the day. This also teaches my son that the first fruits of his day go to The Most High.

Now I know I spoke on the morning praise heavily, but that's to get you in the habit of praising when you first get up, in an effort to keep you in that space throughout the day. However, there still has to be very real effort throughout the day to keep your praise. I know this time in your life is very challenging and I know how it feels to feel like you don't have anything to praise God for because of the hurt and the heavy burden that you're carrying. But the fact that you are up, that you can read this book tells me that your story is not over, and for that alone you should be praising. Like I said earlier, it takes the focus off you, and puts it on the only one who can change your circumstance. So, you ought to get to lifting him up. Learn how to use your voice to provoke action in the Father. He loves you, and he wants a relationship with you. Most importantly, his word specifically tells us "Enter his gates with thanksgiving and into his courts with praise; be thankful unto him and bless his name." (Psalm 100:4) Therefore, learn how to enter the gates of the Kingdom, and how to access the throne room so you can get the Lord to move on your behalf. He shows us very clearly in his word how to come into his presence, and you do that by praise and worship.

The importance of being in his presence are the many things that can happen there. Not only do you get his attention, you draw closer to him, and he is more keen to moving for you. I know it doesn't seem like it now, but I promise you in doing so you will begin to know God on a deeper level because you will begin to see how he operates and how he moves. Pay attention. Your praise can cause things laying of the hands and even prayer cannot. So, make sure you keep your voice, and lift it high no matter what is going on in your life. Keep your praise!

Your praise will be one of the most effective tools you have to get the attention of The Most High and get him to move on your behalf. Your praise will not only confuse the enemy, but it is also a powerful mood booster. Get in the habit of praising God and watch how things begin to move for you.

Do you find it easy to get into a place of praise? Does praise come very natural for you, or does this activity still feel a bit forced?

_____
_____
_____
_____
_____
_____
_____
_____

Can you describe a time you felt the presence of God during a praise session?

_____
_____
_____
_____
_____
_____
_____
_____

How has your praise helped you in this journey?

_____
_____
_____
_____
_____
_____
_____
_____

Some of my go to songs that get me in God's presence are: Vashawn Mitchell's Worship Medley, Lauren Daigle's You Say, and J.J. Hairston's You Deserve It. How do you get into the presence of The Most High, and how have you noticed your spirit reacts when you're in this space?

_____
_____
_____
_____
_____
_____
_____
_____

Affirmation:

I will bless the Lord at all times and his praise shall continually be in my mouth.

The Assembly Line

Stand On IT!

To stand every morning to thank and praise the Lord, and likewise at evening.

1 Chronicles 23:30

Workstation 6

Find Purpose

I know it may be hard to see right now but believe it or not there is purpose in your situation. There is purpose in the pain, purpose in why you're having to go through what you're going through, or went through, and purpose in you. To understand this, you must first understand that The Most High does nothing without a plan. Your destiny was planned before you came into this world (Jeremiah 1:5), and he knew the things you would encounter along the way. He knew the things that would attack you, the choices you would make, and the decisions that you made to land you in some unsavory situations. Yet, he still decided to call your life forth. Understand that. And he called your life forth, because there is something that he wants you to do, that ONLY YOU CAN DO!

Everyone walking the face of this planet has a purpose, and as my daddy says, purpose sustains life. If there is still breath in your body, there is still work for you to get done. Now you may be asking what does all of that have to do with what you're going through now? The truth of the matter is, I can't answer that for you. No one will be able to. It is going to take you, stepping back, getting out of your feelings, and asking God to show you what it is he is trying to get out of you, show you, or do through you. The big thing here is GET OUT OF YOUR FEELINGS!

Let me take a minute to home in on this. As long as you're sitting around playing the blame game, throwing yourself pity parties, and wallowing in your feelings, you are not going to see the bigger picture. Now I am not trying to sound harsh, or insensitive, but the fact of the matter is, where has that gotten you thus far? Has it improved your situation? Has it made you feel better? Have your circumstances changed because of it? I can guarantee you the answer to all three of those questions is no, so get your tail up and find out the purpose behind the pain.

I remember a time before my son's father completely left, and we were still in this phase of his indecisiveness. I was sleeping, and sleeping well might I add, and waking up to an onset of text messages from him where he was just wilding out. He was talking crazy, had called me out of my name, and sent me pictures of other girls comparing me to them. He had sent me messages of guys numbers who were stored in my phone, telling me to be with them. Just all this crazy stuff. It was just so obscene, and something I had never witnessed from him before. It was like my spirit knew something wasn't right because it was too far outside of what I knew his character to be. I said, "Lord, what is wrong with him? Show me what's really going on, or is he really just a nut like this?" I mean, I knew him. I knew he had a temper and I knew that he could trip, but it was something about these messages. He was so angry. It really threw me off. God simply told me, "It's a spirit. It is the spirit of rejection." He said, "The spirit in him is colliding with the spirit in you." I was walking around in my room thinking, "okay so what am I supposed to do with that? What am I supposed to do about that?" At this point in my pregnancy I wasn't too into the whole spiritual aspect of what was going on. I mean, I knew there was a spiritual aspect, and I knew for the most part that there was something going on in the spirit realm, but I wasn't that in tune, and I wasn't deep enough in my relationship and walk with God to determine what it was exactly.

I remember writing down what the Holy Spirit had said, and when I met with my dad for our weekly Starbucks touch base, I told him what happened and what the Holy Spirit told me. My father went on to elaborate about the difference of spirits that were at odds with each other, and before we left, he prayed for my son's father and his family. Now I'm not going to lie, I wasn't in a head space where I really cared about him or his family at that time and I darn sure didn't want to be praying their protection....and let me add, it took a LONG time for me to get in that space. Any who, my father told me that we were at spiritual odds because there were two parties at work here. The Most High God, who is represented in me, and birthing this child was all a part of God's bigger plan. Then there was the enemy, who was moving and having his way in my son's father because he was upset that God's plan was in motion. Again, being in the natural it was very hard to digest all of this without holding my son's father accountable for his actions. Nevertheless, trusting my father and knowing enough about God and the kingdom of light and darkness, I knew what my dad was saying had some validity. I just didn't know to what extent, and truth be told, emotionally I wasn't ready to excuse it under the guise of spiritual odds.

But God! As time went on, I continued to question God and ask him why? Why did I have to go through this, why my child, what's going to happen, what's the point? Although, he still to this day has not told me exactly what is going to happen, I do have a more clear and better understanding of the purpose behind it. Now while I know and believe God did not bring my son's father into my life, he definitely used the relationship, in his sovereignty, to advance His plan for my life. I can look back now and see that me getting pregnant was the catalyst that pushed me deeper into my walk, and on the collision path to my destiny. My pregnancy was my power switch.

Now, all and all we know that God could have got me right where he wanted me in many of different ways, but that's where our free will comes into play. I would venture to say that this was not God's Plan A for my life. I'm sure he had a different idea of how he wanted to get me to my appointed end. But like I'm sure you've heard a thousand times before, God is a gentleman, and he does not force himself upon us. He may nudge us, give us heads ups and promptings when we're making certain moves, or decisions- but all and all he does not decide for us unless we allow him to. So, although he wants us to go a certain way because there may be less heartache and pain, he has already laid out a plan according to the choices and decisions he already knows we're going to make.

This was the case here. He knew I would meet my son's father, he knew he would warn me during the relationship, and he knew I wouldn't listen. It's that simple. The warning was to save me from the pain, but he was prepared for what was going to happen, and he knew it would be the very thing to make me run to him. Think of it like this, when you see your child running with their shoes untied (just stay with me), you warn them like, "stop running before you hurt yourself." Most of the time not going into details about the possibility of tripping over their shoestring and busting their face, you simply say, "stop running." Then BOOM! They bust they head. Are they crying, and all bent out of shape, yes? Are you surprised by this happening, no. You get up, get the First Aid kit, explaining the importance of listening to you, while comforting them until they're ready to get back out there. It's the exact same thing with the Father and us. He didn't want that to happen to you, but he knew it happening to you would draw you to him, and ultimately that's what he wants from all of us.

As long as you stay close to him, he will nurse you. He will heal your wounds. He will show you why it happened, and also show you the root cause of the issue that led you to even be in a place to get in the situation- and that's the underline of what you want to know, and what you want him to remove from you. He will bring exposure and healing to all of it, if you stay under his care. This, however, is a process. It is not an overnight thing, not by a long shot. So be ready to journey, but again, I'm telling you, it's going to be amazing. Only the Father can tell you about yourself, bring healing to you, and change you all at the same time. Hallelujah!

We do not always understand the things that The Most High either takes us through or allows us to go through, but we are not called to understand. We are called to have faith in him, which is essentially just trusting that the God of this world, the God of all the universe loves you enough to keep you in the palm of his hand. God does not allow us to go through significant pain and trauma without there being some sort of purpose for it, or purpose behind the matter. Unfortunately, the hardest part to come to grips with is, oftentimes we won't know the full purpose of a thing until you're coming out or all the way delivered from it. Keep your eyes on God along the way and you will come out, better, and fulfilled. You will also understand why you had to go through it.

I know it was hard to see it at first, but over time, aren't you now able to see things a bit clearer? You probably have a better understanding of what's going on now also. That's what happens when we decide to seek God in the middle of our hell. Even if we don't necessarily like the why, we at least get purpose.

What has God been revealing to you about your situation?

_____
_____
_____
_____
_____
_____
_____
_____

Maybe it hasn't been about your current situation. What has God been revealing to you in general?

_____
_____
_____
_____
_____
_____
_____
_____

What were some of the main questions you had at the beginning of your journey? Have you received any insight, revelation or understanding of any of them?

_____
_____
_____
_____
_____
_____
_____
_____

What was your 'ah ha' moment? What has stood out to you the most?

_____
_____
_____
_____
_____
_____
_____

Have you seen changes not only in yourself, but the people around you?

_____
_____
_____
_____
_____
_____
_____

Affirmation:

I am at peace with God's sovereignty, all things are working together for my good.

Stand On IT!

And we know that in all things God works for the good of those who love him, who have been called according to his purpose.

Romans 8:28

Workstation 7

Let the Holy Spirit Work

Scripture warns us to "quench not the Holy Spirit" (1 Thessalonians 5:19) and so often we hear that and automatically correlate it to ignoring the warnings of the Holy Spirit when it relates to sin, but the job of the Holy Spirit is so much more than talking us out of sinning. However, it is our job to not only recognize movement of the Ruach, but to also allow it to move freely- thus not "quenching" it in any area of our lives.

It is the Holy Spirit (or Ruach Ha'Kodesh) that leads us and guides us throughout and into the changes that the Father is doing in us. The Holy Trinity is brilliant in all its ways, and every entity plays a significant part in ultimately getting you to become the person that you were originally designed to be. The person that you now have to learn how to be, and who is better to show you or guide you, than your designer? Now because you are a spirit filled believer (**Spirit Check:** you are a spirit filled believer, right?) you have been blessed with the gift of God's spirit burning inside of you. The spirit is there to walk you along the way. It is by allowing, listening, and obeying the Ruach of God that you will begin to see the evolution that is taking place in you. Your growth, and evolvement will directly line up with the words, instructions, and prophecies The Most High has been speaking over and into your life.

See now remember I told you from the very beginning that God had a plan, and the pain was for a reason. Nothing God does is just for fun, there is purpose in every movement of God. So now here we are, we've been through the fire. The initial shock of trauma has come and went. Now what? The situation hasn't changed, you're still left with the residuals, but the world hasn't stopped. Life is still going on- which means there's more to the plan, and now we're shifting into the next phase of this thing! See it's now no longer about what happened to you, now we're assessing how what happened to you is propelling you into your future. How is what happened to you going to be used moving forward, in the latter part of God's plan? This is what you should be pondering on now. We dropped the pity party back in chapter six, it is now time to come up and dwell a little higher...you ready?

The Assembly Line

*An assembly line is a progressive process in which parts are added as the semi-finished assembly, or product, moves from workstation to workstation where the parts are added **in sequence** until the <u>final assembly is produced.</u>*

You are being assembled, and it is the work of the Holy Spirit to ensure the proper parts, fillings, and connections are being added to you at each workstation. See at the beginning of the assembly line you were just scattered pieces, fabric, raw material. No shape, no form, no inclination of your potential and purpose. In darkness, without a clue. Then the conveyer belt started, and things began to move, and the movement was highly uncomfortable because there was no clear vision of what was coming, and what the end would be. Just sudden movement. Movement that caused you to jerk a bit, it shifted you, took you out of your comfort zone because you were not in control. You had no authority over the off switch- you were forced to move.

While you were drawing closer to God, following the steps outlined above. The Most High was working on your heart, and spiritually assembling you into the person he needs you to be. Take a look at your life. What different events have taken place? What have been some of your experiences? Are you discerning what part of your journey you are in? Can you recognize how God is working on you, what he is doing, what he is changing, or has already changed?

Workstations

Each workstation signifies a different area of you or something in your life. It is the thing that God is working on at that very moment. It is the area that he is pressing you, reshaping you, and giving you new oil. It is the flavor of the hour that he has decided is not pleasing to his taste buds and will not be digestible to the audience that he is calling you to. These different experiences, characteristics, events, are all different workstations that The Most High is using to tweak things out of you.

At each workstation it is imperative that you understand what is being done, and you cooperate with the Holy Spirit. You may not understand the full reason as to why, or what purpose the work will serve, but you must be open to allowing the Holy Spirit to work- thus not quenching the spirit.

One of the workstations I remember staying on the longest was my temper. When I tell you, I used to have a bit of a temper, and would walk around like a ticking time bomb....it was bad. I was so irritable, so uptight, and just on edge for no reason. I took everything personal, and I didn't like anyone saying anything to me that I didn't want to hear. I remember my mom told me once, people felt like they had to walk on eggshells around me, because they didn't want to say the wrong thing, to set me off. Now initially when she said it, I just thought she was exaggerating a bit, but then my oldest sister seconded what she said, and it was the look on her face when she was talking to me that I knew she felt the same way.

I knew I needed to get my attitude together, but I legitimately didn't know how. I was always so annoyed. People annoyed me, and I swore with everything in me that I wasn't the problem, it was everyone else. It was as if it was from that moment on that Yahuah just began to press on me. I couldn't not think about my responses and reactions to things. Every time someone offended me, or ticked me off and I would respond in my normal fashion, the Holy Spirit would just nag at me like, why'd you say that? You shouldn't have said that. You didn't need to yell like that. Oh, and the worst was, "Did you show God in how you handled that?" Oh my gosh it used to make me feel like.... just get it together Erika, you have to do better.

He continued to give me opportunity after opportunity to respond differently, to tame my tongue, or just not to speak at all. Sometimes I did well, and sometimes I completely bombed. The point is I listened to the voice of the spirit, and I moved at his nudging. By the power of the Holy Spirit I consistently worked to do better, and over the course of three years (yes baby a whole 1095 days!!!) I can boldly say I have come a long way. You can no longer get an immediate hellfire reaction out of me. I now sit back, process, and sit on my anger (just because I don't respond doesn't mean I'm not angered), I simply now have better control of my emotions. It is my understanding that where he is taking me, I cannot be acting a fool, and because I am a representative of him, he will take three years to work that fool right on out of me.

These different experiences have been building character in you. It is through these experiences and being assembled at these workstations that God is molding you. Your attitude is changing, your way of thinking is different. Your perspective is different. You now have a better understanding of the hell you went through, and your view on that situation is a little more positive. You see the light, and you can now rest in God's grace for that thing.

So, you must understand that it is by work of the Holy Spirit, and an obedient heart, that the change is going to happen. Also understand that if God has chosen you to do his will....his will, will be done. The Holy Spirit will lead and guide you along the way. You will know when you are doing right, and when there is something he wants to change. So, don't prolong the process by fighting against it, you'll only end up hurting yourself.

Sometimes the changes in us are so subtle, we don't even recognize the work that has been done. On the other hand, there are very noticeable differences that even others around you can see. All and all we give God the glory and bless him for the work that has been accomplished, but also take the time to applaud yourself for your effort and submission to God's hand in your life.

Have you been able to recognize the workstations you've gone through? Being processed through, do you see the difference they have made in your life?
_____
_____
_____
_____
_____
_____
_____
_____
_____

What has been the workstation you've stayed on the longest, and why?
_____
_____
_____
_____
_____
_____
_____
_____
_____

Allowing The Most High to process you is hard! What has been the most challenging part for you, and how have you overcome it?

_____
_____
_____
_____
_____
_____
_____
_____

Taking a moment to relish in your growth, what are you most proud of, and what has been your biggest accomplishment?

_____
_____
_____
_____
_____
_____
_____
_____

How does knowing that God is pressing you to make you better, and lead you to a better future help you stay on path day to day? Does it help at all?

_____
_____
_____
_____
_____
_____
_____
_____

Affirmation:

I am God's workmanship, created to showcase his glory!

The Assembly Line

Stand On IT!

For we are His workmanship, created in Christ Jesus unto good works, which God hath beforehand ordained, that we should walk in them.

Ephesians 2:10

Workstation 8

The Final Assembly

Okay, the work has been done. There's definitely a change in you, and you didn't even notice it at first, did you? But over time, by the work of the Holy Spirit, things that once interested you, no longer. The activities you used to love, you no longer feel the need to partake in, and the way that you used to act, you no longer act. There's something different about you. It's cool, but it's weird all at the same time. It's really quite amazing when you think about it. See what can happen when you allow yourself to grow? Notice I said allow, because you had a choice, and you made the right one. Good for you.... but now what? Things are feeling a bit different, and you're not quite sure of what to do with yourself. Trust me I totally understand. It's like once you get to this place of "growth", where the things of your past no longer interest or serve you, you can almost feel lost. It's almost as if you don't know what to do. Like you're missing something, but what you know you can get, is not really what you want, and maybe you're not quite sure of what you want so you find yourself dabbling in what you know. Or you know exactly what you want but worst of all, it's out of your hands. *Deep sigh.* I know this all too well.

At this point in my journey I was at a place in my walk with God where I just wanted more and more truth. God was revealing and showing so much to me I just couldn't get enough. However, there were times when I wanted a break, and I wanted to do other things. Like outside of God. Lol! Not like that, but you know, take a study break- get a life and do something. That's when I realized, I didn't really know who I was any more. I mean, I know that may sound a bit dramatic, but outside of the party girl that I once was- who was I? My past identity was wrapped up in my party lifestyle, but here we are five years later and it's like okay? Now what to do for fun? What do I like? What are my interests?

Now I know for some of you your past identity was something different. Maybe it was drugs, promiscuity, or maybe your identity has been defined by pain- but regardless of what it was, where does that leave you now? Who are you now? Have you figured that out and if so, have you accepted the new you?

The New You

Who are you? Who is the person that The Most High has been revealing to you? Have you figured that out yet? Have you been listening to the Spirit? Following instruction, doing what The Most High has told you to do? So, who has He been putting together? What changes have you noticed about yourself, what do you do differently? What is your story? Where has He taken you from and delivered you to?

You're holding a lot. You're growing, and evolving...all the while carrying the initial heaviness of what happened...how many years ago? The very thing that set this thing is motion is still very much present and real in your life. But because of the sheer fact that you CHOSE to keep your eyes on God, drawing nigh to him, and obeying his word and instruction- he has blessed you, right alongside the very thing that was meant to curse you. HALLELUJAH!

I was doing my thing. I was raising my child, who was just blossoming with the most beautiful spirit. I was advancing in my career, climbing the corporate ladder. I got two promotions over the course of 2/12 years, with a promotion on the horizon. The Most High had blessed me with a cute little cottage style apartment for me and my baby. I mean we were happy, genuinely happy. I was blessed...but I didn't fully recognize it.

It is imperative that you not only recognize, but rest in your blessings. Rest in the New You. Never losing sight of what the Father has done, too focused on the unknown ahead, and what you left behind. Now it's easy to say that once you begin to grow you won't go back, but before you get too high- remember, that quiet time of the unknown can get real lonely, real frustrating, real tiresome, and real disappointing, really quick. Making it easy to grow weary from the continual working, pushing, and stretching of yourself.

I can speak passionately about this because roundabout this point in my life, I didn't take the time to enroll in courses, or get into some groups, or do anything that would nurture my new self, and the path I was headed down. Although looking back, I was prompted by the Holy Spirit to do so numerous times. I found myself entertaining what I knew. Only to a certain extent but hindering enough. I didn't start back partying, but I did start hanging out a lot again. The problem wasn't so much in the hanging out, it was more that it fostered behaviors that were previously broken. For instance, me smoking, and because I don't smoke without drinking, I began to drink more also. Some may say, well that's not so bad, and well, it's not the worst thing...but it did aid in further poor decision making. I began wanting to hang out and drink more than I wanted to sit down and study. Don't get me wrong, I still prayed, I worshipped, I talked to God throughout the day- all that. However, what was most needed from me during this time, was alone time in the presence of God. I should have been increasing my study time, instead of increasing my new "party time." Truthfully, had I raised my level of commitment during that time, my longing to do more outside of God would have decreased. He would have continued to take me higher, and show me more of his plan, and I would have been able to find peace in that.

Heed my warning, and do not get caught up in things that do not serve you. It is so very easy for us to fall off track and be distracted by things that are comfortable to us. This is one of the enemy's greatest weapons. Remember, it was not comfort that caused you to grow, but just the opposite. Do not get this far, and let boredom, impatience, and laziness cause you to stay in this space longer than what you need to.

For biblical reference, this phase in your life, The Final Assembly, can be compared to your wilderness experience. Really, the whole journey has been your wilderness, but you are now at the place where it is just about time to enter the Promise Land. The wilderness was never meant to be comfortable, it is your escape from your past to the new thing that God has laid out in front of you. Do not, be like the Children of Israel, and die in your wilderness never seeing the Promised Land.

The Most High has been forming you and sustaining you. So, it is important that you begin to do things that are going to nurture and support the new form. The most important being your alone time with the Father. At this stage in your journey it is time for you to increase your level of commitment. LEVEL UP! You should be reading and studying more. You should be spending increased amounts of time in God's presence, learning him and his plan. Next you need to find habits, activities, and forums that express and strengthen the new you.

I encourage you, during this time of finalization, the voice of the spirit may not be as loud, and that's just because he's putting the finishing touches on you. The Holy Spirit has been working. You've been working hard, doing your part on the outside, and the Holy Spirit has been doing away at you on the inside. The sooner you align and accept the final product, the sooner you will be able to see and operate in his completed work. Look back and see how far The Most High has brought you. Everything about you is different. You are better, you are wiser, your discernment is on point, and your gifts have been perfected. Most importantly, your relationship with the Father has grown and strengthened. You are a completely different being.... you're better. You have finally been fully assembled.

Praise God and rest in his glory. For soon it will be time to move.

You've been walking this thing out, and although it hasn't been easy, you haven't given up. You are different. You look and feel different and in the midst of everything going on around you God himself has completed a seamless transition in your spirit, your emotions, and even your thought process. You're no longer your old self, and you're coming into an acceptance of the New You!

Looking back on where it all began, how do you feel to finally be in this space?

_____
_____
_____
_____
_____
_____
_____
_____

What are some of the more visible changes that you're now able to see? What are some of the changes that you were once overlooking?

_____
_____
_____
_____
_____
_____
_____
_____

What has been the most challenging part of this process for you? On the contrary, what has been the easiest?

_____
_____
_____
_____
_____
_____
_____
_____

Do you feel like you finally have the proper perspective of your situation? If so, how has the change in your perspective allowed you to be at peace with what you've gone through?

_____
_____
_____
_____
_____
_____
_____
_____

Finally, free and no longer bound to your emotional trauma, how has your growth changed your outlook on your future?

_____
_____
_____
_____
_____
_____
_____
_____

Affirmation:

The old things have passed away, and I am a new creature in Christ.

Stand On IT!

Finally, be strong in the Lord and in his mighty power. Put on the full armor of God, so that you can take your stand against the devil's schemes.

Ephesians 6:10-11

Shipping and Handling

Time to Move

This stage requires action, and that means you! The work of the spirit is done, now it's time to put that work in to action in the natural. What has God been asking of you? What instructions has he given you? You need to know this, because it's time to move.

Probably about a year after I had my child, and that's a huge estimate, The Most High began telling me that He blessed me with the ability to write. He continually told me, although I've tried before, this time would be different if I wrote a book. He wanted me to write a book, this book actually. He wanted me to document my story and show what I did to get out of a very traumatizing place in my life. He wanted to use me to draw others nearer to him, and for him to do that through me, I needed to tell my story.... most importantly, I needed to be obedient. Well this scared me a bit, and I'm not going to lie, I sat on it for a while before taking any action. Eventually, I said let's do it and I began to write. It has taken me a total of three years to write this book, to complete the work.

Most of the delay in completing this book had to do with fear and discouragement, which I believe is normal, and all apart of the process. However, just like I said in Chapter 1: GOD HAS A PLAN, and we must trust it. Now, you're being asked to trust God in a different way, for a different thing in your life, but you must believe just as he got you through the trauma, he will make you triumphant. All you have to do is take the first step, and let the Holy Spirit lead you from there.

The Most High has been speaking to you throughout this journey. He has been molding you, shaping you, and pressing you, to push you into that thing that he originally called you to. What has he been telling you to do? Are you to write a book? Start a business? Open a school? Change jobs? Move? What instructions has The Most High been giving you, because it is now time to move on them. Your ability to follow instruction and move on the word of the Lord is directly tied to your destiny and promise. God did not start your assembly just to put you together and leave you there. The product that has been created has a destiny, and someone is waiting on your delivery. You must do the work. Your destiny depends on it. Surely you didn't go through all of this in vain.

I knew it was time to move when I began to see all the pieces to my next level make their way in front of me. It was as if God was dropping hints to me. He was showing me everything that we were moving into. The Most High began to show me the next steps in my career, what my next move would be, and the next thing I'd be doing. It was everything I wanted, everything I had been praying for. Here it was, and he was telling me, you are about to have it all, but you've got to move. You've got to complete that thing I've instructed you to do. It's the final piece.

Now because I had been dragging my feet for so long, again, mainly because I was allowing fear to hold me back from moving forward, The Most High was done playing with me. He told me very clearly that the book had to be done by a specific date, and he also made it very clear of what would happen if it wasn't. This scared my butt right into action, because what I didn't want to happen, was me missing out on my promise, because of fear. Let me tell you, there is nothing worse than realizing that YOU are your biggest hold back. It's one thing when you have other circumstances and people to blame stuff on, but when God brings you through, and creates a lane just for you....and you don't move? That is all on you, and there is no excuse for that!

So, let me tell you what happens when you don't move, and hopefully this will encourage you to do what you need to do. See God has been taking good care of you. He has been keeping you just as he promised in the beginning when you decided to trust him. You've received a few blessings and have always had everything you needed. That was because of the alignment, you and God were rocking together, but when you heed not the instruction of The Most High, things can get really uncomfortable. At this point in your journey it is time to elevate. It is time for you to bloom, and the key to you blooming is doing that thing that God has been telling you to do. The result of not blooming when you are meant to, is discomfort. By now, you are too big to stay where you are. That is why God is calling your forth to blossom. If you choose to keep yourself tucked away, you will not only miss the opportunity to blossom, but you are going to be very uncomfortable in the meantime.

People tend to have a misconception of God and discomfort. At this point in your walk you shouldn't, but let me further explain. The Most High allows, orchestrates, and uses discomfort to move us into an area that he wants us to be in. Just as he allowed, orchestrated, or used your experience to get you here. He will do it again if need be, and why go through that? For me my thought process was, this was already too painful. I wasn't willing to see what I would have to go through due to my disobedience. I didn't want to have to see how uncomfortable it would get because I was out of the will of God. Being out of the will of God is what caused me to be in this situation to begin with. Fear wasn't worth it for me.

You too should be ready to go into your next level. You should want to see what all of this was for, and you should definitely want to see your reward. Oh, I never mentioned your reward?

The Most High is a rewarder of those who surrender their heart, will, and life to him. He is going to reward you for your hard work, and he is going to compensate you for the pain, hurt and heartache that you went through. He is going to bless you for your obedience and faithfulness to him. You will get all of that, and all of that is tied to your destiny. God wants to do a work in your life that is inconceivable to you at this time, but you have to be willing. He has been dropping hints and showing you snippets of what's in store for you. For some of you, he has given you a promise. Trust him, he is asking you to continue to trust him and move. The faith in your movement, will bring forth your new dimension. This is your time.

It is time for your next level! And all you have to do is walk in it. Walk in that thing that God has been calling you to do. The thing that He has placed on your heart. Now that He has completed His perfect work in you, He wants you to be a blessing unto someone else. Are you ready?

Has God given you vision into the next level? Do you see where He is taking to you?

_____
_____
_____
_____
_____
_____
_____
_____
_____

What is the thing that God has placed on your heart to do? Have you started on it? If not, what is it that's holding you back?

_____
_____
_____
_____
_____
_____
_____
_____

How're you feeling about this new beginning? Are you ready and excited? Has anxiety or fear gripped you? What are your true feelings and how have you been handling it?

_____
_____
_____
_____
_____
_____
_____
_____

Now that you know where you're going, have you asked God to show you how to get there? Write the vision.

_____
_____
_____
_____
_____
_____
_____
_____

Write out a list of the things you want to accomplish in this season.

_____
_____
_____
_____
_____
_____
_____
_____

Affirmation:

I am walking in purpose, aligned with and in the center of God's will for my life.

Stand On IT!

You did not choose me, but I chose you and appointed you that you should go and bear fruit and that your fruit should abide

John 15:16

Signed, Sealed, Delivered

Thrive

Thrive (/THrīv/) -
1. (of an animal, child, or plant) to grow or develop well or vigorously; flourish
2. prosper; to be fortunate or successful

Blossom and Be! The Most High was able to get something out of you, pressed oil. A new anointing. Now, HE is ready to elevate you. Yahuah said, "Blossom and Be! You are now ready for the next level, for your culmination has come, and it is time you arise."

I was riding in my car coming back from an unexpected doctor's appointment, and Yahuah began to speak to me. He began to tell me; the time was now. He has tried and tested me, and because I stayed with him, it was now time for the promise. "Elevation is here, you have shifted, and everything I promised you is for now." Glory be to God! Imagine my excitement.

The Most High is a rewarder of good faith, and because of your faith and obedience he has brought you to a place of promise. Elevation is here. Your life is getting ready to take off, and God is saying to you today, **"Walk in It!** In order for you to receive what I have for you, you must simply walk in it, and you will thrive."

Affirmation:

I am walking in the abundance of The Most High!

The Finished Product
(Epilogue)

YOUR BROKENNESS WAS FOR YOUR GOOD!

A new heart also will I give you, and a new spirit will I put within you: and I will take away the stony heart out of your flesh, and I will give you an heart of flesh.

Ezekiel 36:26

And I will give them an heart to know Me, that I am the Lord: and they shall be My people, and I will be their God: for they shall return unto Me with their whole heart.

Jeremiah 24:7

Do not just push to survive but push to thrive! God wants to do so much more with you! Do not get stuck in your brokenness, in that wilderness! You were never meant to stay there! Keep pushing! God is going to get something out of you and elevate you, but you have to give him something to work with. Get out of survival mode, God said "Seek ye first the Kingdom of God and his righteousness, and all these things will be added to you." (Matthew 6:33) You do not have to just survive he will provide! Seek the Lord and all of his ways in all that you do, seek purpose and push through! Get out of your brokenness and thrive! Take that dead thing and speak life into it. The Lord said, "Prophesy to these bones and say to them, 'Dry bones, hear the word of the Lord!" (Ezekiel 37:4) Your circumstance has changed, you have changed, and you are better. To God be the glory. That thing was designed to work in your favor- WORK IT!

You can't work it if you're still crying over it, you can't work it if you're still mad about it, it won't work if you're still sitting around bitter about it. You have to look at that thing and say, "God where are we going with this?" "What part do I need to play while you turn this around in my favor for your glory?" He will do it! That is why he is God the Most High! Thee exalted, the most powerful and almighty one. He is bigger than what you're going through, and he will be exalted through this process.

Remember, God is a sovereign God, which means he is even God over your circumstance. You were never meant to deal with it alone. God is not through with you yet! Get your life and your power back! Go after your destiny! And if within this process you have a beautiful child to show for it like me, then pack the kid(s) and bring them along! Soon you'll be shouting IT WAS GOOD THAT I WAS AFFLICTED!

Yahuah has you! Don't ever forget that, he tells us 365 times in the bible to not be afraid-meaning keep going, DAILY! It's not going to overtake you! He knows what he's doing, it's time you trust him and push through!

Bless

He Gives Beauty for Ashes

Isaiah 63:1

ABOUT THE AUTHOR

Erika Danielle Neal is the founder of Erika, Speak Easy, a ministry dedicated to helping people not get stuck when trials arise, but rather use those trials as stepping blocks to get to their God-given destiny. Through her own suffering, she developed a clear understanding of how The Most High wanted her to respond and produce out of what she was going through. Understanding why Yahuah allows us to suffer through heartache, heartbreak, trials and tribulations, Erika has devoted herself to helping people get her same understanding, grow spiritually, and remain unmoved and steadfast.

Erika Danielle Neal lives in Long Beach, California, and is the mother of a boisterous little boy lovingly nicknamed Lucky. You can get in contact with her directly on her blogsite at www.erikaspeakeasy.com.

www.ingramcontent.com/pod-product-compliance
Lightning Source LLC
Chambersburg PA
CBHW051657040426
42446CB00009B/1179